Star Child

by Kay Goldstein

For Zach & Julie Goodyear,

Wishing you joy in every season!

K. Goldstein

VINEYARD STORIES
Edgartown, Massachusetts

Volume Copyright ©2012 Kay Goldstein

Published by:
Vineyard Stories
52 Bold Meadow Road
Edgartown, Massachusetts 02539
508-221-2338
www.vineyardstories.com

Library of Congress Control Number: 2012935262
ISBN: 978-0-9849136-1-9

Book Design: Jill Dible, Atlanta, Georgia

Editor: Jan Pogue, Vineyard Stories

Printed in China

For Katherine and Max

Heaven

Millennia of light and heat, the birth of planets, the cooling of suns, the unfolding of lifetimes, the thinking, the being, the seeing, the knowing. All this she witnessed in her heavenly orbit. She embraced each moment of light and dark, each transformation of swirling gases, each clash and crumbling of brittle crusts, each volcanic handprint and frozen ocean, each a part of her and she a part of each, all connected by the caressing wind of the great Cosmic Breath. As she dove into the atmosphere of the blue planet, surrendering to the fire that consumed her, she kept deep in her memory all she had known, the light song of her life. And this, melting in the heat, shaped the fine clear crystal within her.

Earth

She stood in the waving green meadow and took it all in: the stalks of grass moving in the curved palm of the wind; the gentle hum of a wayward bee easing first away, then closer to touch her; the amber of the sun's bright globe painting her face and arms; the taste of lavender in the air slipping past her lips and melting on her tongue. And she felt such joy that every part of her being filled up, and being filled, welled over as tears.

The star child had planted herself in this earth meadow seven winters earlier, the soul-seed of a dying star burning its path through a midnight sky. Only the sparrows and cottontails, fooled from their sleep by the brilliant light, witnessed the last hiss of steam and the fading glow of the crystal as it slipped beneath the silver snow carpet.

The child tugged her feet from the grip of the moist earth. Her skin was translucent, like the pale roots of a plant. The blue lines of her veins decorated her wrists and arms and at her temple where her red hair began its twisting journey to her waist. Meadow flowers circled her head and trailed down each shoulder. Her garment was all shades of light, changing in the sun and shadows so that one moment it appeared torn from a sunset and in the next as rippling sea foam.

Stretching her arms to the sun and breathing in the clear air, she thanked the universe for her life and made a small bow of respect to the wisdom embedded in the crystal she carried within her. Following its guiding currents, she moved instinctively toward a small rise in the meadow hill.

She walked to the winding edges of the forest where buttercups brushed the moss and ferns. Wild raspberries and blueberries, which she picked at the edge of the hill, slid in their own bittersweet juice down her throat. She nibbled dandelion, spearmint, wild onion, and the spicy leaves of watercress plucked from the waters of a brook. Ahead she could hear the faint lapping of the ocean's surf as it gently stirred the glistening pebbles at the shore. She climbed the next hill where the grasses mingled with stands of wild sea oats.

It was there, where the forest and meadow met the dunes of the shore, that she saw the weather-worn cottage nestled into the hillside. A narrow porch stretched across the front. Its roof, supported by four simple pine columns, hovered between a planked wooden floor and the broad blue sky. A rocker moved with the brushstrokes of the breeze, and a wooden door, standing half-opened, beckoned her to the threshold.

She peered inside and saw a narrow stairway and walls lined with earthen-colored jars and pottery crocks. A cushioned chair waited by the fireplace. A wooden table, draped with oilcloth in the center of the room, held a vase of flowers, an open book, and a squat teapot whose glaze had cracked from the heat of steaming teas. Another door opened upon an iron bed layered with quilts that covered all but the softly curled gray hair of a sleeping old man.

The star child walked slowly to the man's bedside and reached her hand to his forehead. She could feel a fever there that was whirling his mind and tangling his dreams, slowing his breath to a shallow sigh. She placed her other hand on his heart, closed her eyes, and felt the rapid beat begin to slow and steady. Within her own chest, a sweet vibration increased, becoming clearer and sending its waves to open her voice to a wordless song of healing. Then her small hands, trembling with the energy of the current, soothed the flame of the man's fever. The girl stood close, her warm hands resting a while longer upon the head and chest of the man's peaceful form. She felt the kindness of his heart and bowed, thankful for the healing.

She then peered around the room, curious about the things she saw that were all wondrous and new to her. She touched the lace of the curtains and felt the softness of the rug under her bare feet. She fingered the teeth of a wooden comb resting on the table near the bed. Finally she seated herself at a chair near the man's bedside.

The star child was dozing when the man opened his eyes. Around them the evening sun, slanting through the window of the bedroom, cast long golden footprints on the floor. They both heard the door swing open and the sound of someone hurrying toward the bedroom. A tiny, wizened woman was startled by what she saw. Only a few hours earlier she had hurried to fetch a tonic from the village in the hope of saving her ailing husband, yet now he sat up wide-eyed and alert, no longer gripped by fever and pain.

"Dearest! I thought I had lost you." The woman spoke breathlessly as she crossed the room to touch the old man's hand and kiss his face.

"I am well," he replied softly as he gazed at her face close to his. "I didn't know where I was. I felt like I was in an oven, then floating in the sky. And then . . ."

The man and woman both turned to the child, now awake, seated by his bed. The sunlight behind her head, bathing her hair in daffodil light, made the old woman think of places just beyond her mind's eye that she knew but could not see. Was she an angel?

"Who are you, child?" the woman asked.

"I came from the meadow beyond the forest," she said, pointing her finger. "I am new here, you see."

"But where do you *live*, my dear?" asked the old man gently.

"I only know that I am here now. If it is elsewhere I belong, I don't know where that might be. Perhaps I should go look," the child replied as she began to rise from the chair.

"Wait!" they cried in unison. "Stay here. It is getting late to be traveling about," offered the old woman. The couple was baffled by the child and by the hypnotic beauty of her voice and what sounded like the faint tinkle of bells that punctuated her speech. Transfixed, they opened their hearts and home to the star child.

The couple cleared a cozy corner of the cabin's loft. The round window above the bed opened to the meadow hills and the sounds of the ocean surf beyond. The star child, whom they called Terra because she said she grew out of the earth, loved this corner of the world. She also came to love the dear couple who taught her the ways of their earthly home.

The old woman took delight in making a doll for her and teaching her to embroider the doll's apron. Terra begged the woman to teach her a new song each day, and soon the sounds of the girl's singing could be heard as she played about the garden or in the loft before she fell asleep. The child found joy and enchantment in each new discovery—the taste of a crisp apple, the colors of the garden flowers, the aroma of the old woman's soup cooking on the hearth. The couple, watching the child, began to find sweetness in even the most common pieces of their life.

It was easy for Terra to wind her way into the old man's heart. She followed him about, watching and helping him with his work. He was patient, showing Terra how to carve wood, catch fish, and turn the wooden bowls that he took to market to sell. They even plowed the fields together, with little Terra astride the big mare. He played tricks on her, too, pretending to use the wrong tool when he polished the surface of a bowl just to see if she would notice. And she teased him back, hiding his chisel or the measuring stick when she knew he'd be wanting it.

"Terra, darling, do you think the gremlins have been here again? I can't seem to find my hammer," he would say, scratching his head and giving her a wink.

One day, while he searched about his workbench in the shed, Terra asked, "Papa, where do you go when you take your sack of bowls over the hill?"

The man stopped, his back stiffening a bit. His head turned from her as he replied, "I go to town, to a market to sell them."

"Oh," she said, trying to imagine what a town and a market looked like. "Are there little ones in the town? Can I go with you to see?"

"Are you not happy? We all have fun together, don't we?"

"Oh yes, I do love it here," she began. "But . . . I want to go there, too!"

"We'll see, my dear. Why don't you go fetch us some water and some apples from the cellar at the cottage?"

Dawdling along the path, Terra glanced back and saw the old man leave the shed and walk a narrow path into the woods. She turned to follow at a distance. She briefly lost sight of him, and then suddenly he was ahead of her. Kneeling in front of a cairn of smooth stones, he was pulling weeds away from them and the space in front of the marker outlined in small white rocks. She saw the shaking of his shoulders as he bent to the ground and then heard a sound so forlorn from him that it seemed to rend the forest air.

That night after Terra had fallen asleep in the loft, the old man spoke to his wife in a low voice: "Terra wants to go with us to market. We can't keep her locked up here forever."

Startled and frightened by his words, his wife spoke sharply, "What would you have us do? We have to protect her from the others. They will know she is different. Even that dress that she wears will mark her. They will think there is witchcraft about."

"Dear one," he replied softly, resting his hand upon hers. "We are getting old. Who would care for her if something happened to us? She has to know how to live and get along in the world. We can't be here forever."

The old woman got up and turned to the pots in the sink, scouring them with a wire brush. The water was scalding, but she reached in again and again. "She's come back to us," she said in a voice strained and cracking, her face twisted in pain. "I lost them. But I won't lose her."

The memories of a distant time grabbed her. She heard the wailing of villagers as the news of the shipwreck broke across the town like a rogue wave. She saw the fire and stones cast upon a lone woman retreating into the darkening forest. And then, when she thought there could be nothing left to pain her, she remembered the momentary glimpse of her only child born but never to live.

She stepped to the door, lingering a moment, then leaning her forehead against the frame. At last she said firmly, "We will take the child with us next week. I will prepare her."

The old woman set about sewing Terra a coat and hat and apron of coarse linen. She made a new dress and told Terra she would be wearing it to town. Terra reluctantly put the new dress on, then turned to see herself in the mirror. "I like my own dress. It is so sparkling. It is like I feel inside. Why can't I wear it?"

The woman reasoned sweetly with her, "It's just that it is not what the others will be wearing, and you wouldn't want folks staring at you and thinking you were a bit strange in the head, now, would you, dear?"

But Terra, who had already noticed that she didn't act or think the same as the old ones, reached for the shimmering garment that she loved. The woman, tugging the dress away from her, brought her face close to Terra's and whispered, "Someone might see you in it and steal you." Terra's eyes were wide with fear as she saw the dress placed in the bottom of a chest, the heavy lid covering its sparkling light. When Terra wanted to look at it once again and reached for the lid, the old woman grabbed her wrist and held it firmly. "This is best," she said, her voice strained and cold. Terra forced a slow nod when she saw the hardness of the woman's face. She turned away and cried.

On market day the three set out for the village. Terra, squirming a bit in her stiff new clothes, could not contain her excitement. But she also noticed a ripple of fear that would slip through her, and she gripped the hands of the old ones as she walked between them.

Finally, the three crested the last steep hill to the village. Just as they reached the top, they came upon a horse standing near a small boy lying motionless among the brambled roses and wildflowers decorating the roadside. The old man dropped his rattling sack of bowls as they hurried to the boy. They saw a large red gash across his forehead and the oddly bent shape of his leg crumpled beneath him.

The star child cried out as she felt the boy's pain. The old couple tried to stop her, but she broke free and knelt by the boy's side, urged on by the pulsing deep in her heart. She gently straightened and held his leg, then moved to wave her hands above the gash on his forehead. Soon the boy stirred and opened his eyes.

"Rest a moment," she whispered.

The old man and woman saw that the boy was healed. Before he fully regained his senses, they hurried Terra away, fearful of the power she held. They did not go on to the village that day but turned back to the safety of their cottage, never speaking of what they had seen. The star child's delight in seeing the boy healed turned cold within her. In the days and months afterward, thinking that she had done something terribly wrong, Terra waved away each new pulse of the crystal. And it was not long before she lost all memory, and even her dreams of her faraway home.

Terra spent her days doing her chores and staying close to the cottage. Sometimes she wandered back to the meadow or climbed high into a tree to sit and watch the ocean. She found solace in those places and the faint familiar feeling of another time and place free of the unspoken boundaries of her life. Once, she even crawled inside the chest, nestling in the dulled shimmer of the dress.

Whenever the old people noticed she was gone, they would call to her. She hid, watching them hunt for her. When they looked away, she would race back to the cottage where they soon returned weary from their search. "Didn't you hear us calling, Terra?" Their voices, sharp and angry, betrayed the fear they felt. And she, who had come unafraid to this place, began to wrap fear about her like a woolen cloak.

On some nights Terra stole into the garden to lay among the straight rows of cabbages and corn or tender pea shoots, watching the luna moths flutter against the moonlight and the stars. She felt as fixed in the earth as the plants about her and knew that even here, as elsewhere in her life, a single stray vine would be pruned and pulled away.

She began falling asleep there, curled among the vegetables, only to be found the next morning by the old woman, her face frantic. The elders began locking the front door with its heavy brass key to keep her safely and properly in her bed. The sound that awakened her was no longer the twitter of the birds but the turning of the metal lock at morning's light.

Sea

*F*rolicking in the moon-dazzled surface of their sea home, five dolphins marveled at the sight of the falling star. They watched the fire split into two pieces high in the indigo heaven, each mapping its own path, one falling to earth and one crashing into the frigid sea.

The dolphins circled the glowing crystal and followed it until it came to rest upon the white sand of the ocean bottom. With their tails, they spun a seaweed cradle. They sang songs of cresting waves, the moonlit dance of foam, lullabies in the endless rhythm of the sea. They kept watch over their treasure, transfixed by its gentle rhythmic currents stroking their skin. The dolphins brought gifts of coral and scallops, pearls and tortoiseshell and sea-worn glass in pastel hues as they waited through the tidal seasons.

A child grew there in the ocean bed, taking his colors from his watery womb, the brown of driftwood to his hair and the green of sea moss and luminous plankton to color his eyes. The coral and gray of beach rocks and shells burnished his skin. He wore an iridescent garment that shimmered like sea spray in the sun. A ring of shell and sea glass graced his neck, just above that place close to his heart that held the crystal. After many seasons, it was the time of the full moon, and the dolphins again circled their precious one. Touching their noses beneath the star child, they lifted him joyfully to the surface of the turquoise sea and placed him carefully on a large flat rock near the shore.

The boy began his first day as a human on the earth hearing the roar of the surf against a rocky ledge, and the fading songs of the dolphins as they slipped beneath the ocean surface. Gazing at the wondrous sight of this world around him, he bowed his head in thanks.

The boy spent many days near the sea rock, diving from its high cliffs, laughing as the waves chased him ashore, and exploring the moss-covered caves that the ocean had carved. He gathered seaweed, mussels, and crabs in tidal pools and played with the fishes and turtles that nipped at his toes. He wandered the meadow hill nearby and lay with his ear upon the golden grass, his body stretched against the ground. He heard earthworms tunneling beneath the dirt and the earth itself breathing beneath him, growing plants, trees, and the tiny roots that sustained all. He cradled himself there, in that fertile ground so different from his sea home.

On the night of the next full moon, he looked down and saw his face mirrored in a tiny pool of water formed among the rocks. He studied his face and eyes and wondered if there were others like him, who were different from the fishes but of the sea no less. He knew then that he did not wish to live alone.

The very next morning, as he wandered toward the meadow above the rock, he came face to face with Terra. She dropped the basket of shells she was collecting, startled not only by his sudden appearance but also by the way her heart leaped in joy when she saw him. She felt certain that she knew him, but she could not name the place of their meeting. They both stood still, staring for many moments. A gull's sharp cry shook them from their trance, and each, suddenly aware of themselves, shyly looked away. Glancing back again, Terra noticed his shimmering clothing, its familiar light twisting together a deep grief and wonderment within her. It was the same as she had once worn. She quickly looked away again. Finally, she stammered, "Are you lost?"

"Lost? I don't know whether I am lost or not. I live down there," he replied, pointing to the beach. "Come, I'll show you," he said eagerly.

Terra stood still, her eyes cast downward. Suddenly, he reached for her hand. She drew back in surprise as a familiar surge of energy went straight into her heart. Catching her breath, she slowly followed.

The young man heard Terra's tentative steps behind him; whenever her eyes rested upon him, he felt a piercing like a single ray of the sun. When they reached the open stretch of beach, he ran for the waves. Terra resumed picking up more shells for her basket. The boy began to gather some for her as he watched from a distance. He felt she had seen something in him that he did not understand and that she could not hide from him.

Soon they walked along together and would run from the skittering crabs and the waves of the incoming tide that caught their feet. The boy began doing handstands in the sand, falling into the waves. Terra collapsed laughing into the sand and watched. Sitting there, she noticed a heart-shaped stone and put it into her pocket.

They walked until they found themselves at the sea rock. "Look at my turtle friend," said the boy, pointing to a little pool of water and watching for Terra's reaction. They both stared at their reflections together, his open-eyed and curious and hers soft and shy. Terra reached into the water to stir it about, and the ripples first scattered then melded their features so that they could not tell one from the other.

Terra shared the bread and cheese she carried in her apron pocket, tearing off small pieces and feeding him like one of the birds at her window. He had never tasted such foods and savored the new flavors. They leaned back against the rock and watched the sun's glitter on the sea. Their hands found their way to each other's, and their fingers entwined and held tight.

The boy felt great contentment but also something unsettling that he could not name.

"What do you hide from me?" he suddenly asked.

But Terra did not answer what she now knew to be the truth. She answered only, "There is pain in both the telling and the holding."

The boy did not press her, for he felt the darkness in her silence. Closing his eyes, he saw the picture of an old wooden trunk closed tight with only the smallest rays of light escaping through the lock. He looked again at her and placed his arms gently about her.

Terra heard the distant calls of the old couple.

"Who's that?" the boy asked, jumping up to look about.

"Shhh, hide behind that rock," whispered Terra as she pulled the boy out of sight. I must go now. Please, please, they must not see you. I'll come back tomorrow. Wait. Wait here for me." Reaching into her pocket, she pulled out the heart-shaped stone and placed it in his hand as she turned and hurried toward the cottage.

Terra did not speak of the boy. She knew she could not explain the gladness she had felt or why she had to return to him again. Back at the cottage she felt her stomach knotting as she thought of the garment he wore and of his question about what she was hiding. She felt that she must tell him what she knew.

She daydreamed through her remaining chores and dawdled over dinner. "I saw rain clouds coming over the big cliff," she offered as they washed the dishes. "Won't the ground be too wet to plant tomorrow?"

The old woman, lips pursed, looked intently at the girl. "Now, what's gotten into you, dearie? You know we've got to get these seeds in the ground before the moon changes."

Terra did not sleep much that night. She would be trapped at the cottage for a whole day, maybe more, and she was afraid the boy might come looking for her. She dragged herself wearily from the loft at the sounds of breakfast and then hurried downstairs. She worked very hard that day, planting, hoeing, and helping the old man with the plow. She desperately wanted to be done and get to the beach, but the old ones set a snail-like pace. It was dark when they finished.

Early the next morning, Terra tiptoed quietly down the stairwell and slipped through an open window. She hurried to the shore, climbing upon the giant sea rock just as the sun began to lighten the sky. Not seeing the boy, she edged higher and scanned the narrow beach that widened steadily with the outgoing tide. In the distance she saw a lazy curl of smoke. She scrambled down to the sand and ran in that direction.

As she reached the craggy shelf that separated her from where she had seen the smoke, her heart froze. Terra saw a fishing boat moored in the depths and a small skiff loaded with fishermen casting off from shore. At the rear of the line of men, she saw the boy. He hesitated, glancing repeatedly back to the beach. Terra stood, her fists clenched. As she tried to call to him, her voice, seized by fear, was but a whisper.

Terra watched as the men climbed aboard their vessel and set sail beyond the ring of the harboring cliffs. She brushed away tears as she climbed down and headed home again, a lone seagull sweeping ahead of her down the beach.

The men who work their nets and backs against the roar of the sea know of sights and sounds and stories that might appear strange to others with less need for magic. Perhaps it is the danger lurking in pounding waves, or the stealth of an unexpected fog, or the disconnected feeling that haunts sailors adrift on a wide ocean that makes them understand things not easily explained.

When the lad, decorated in the colors of the sea, had wandered down the long beach alone, without a boat in sight or even a sack of provisions, the fishermen held their fear and speech in check and said nothing. Instead they offered the young stranger some bread, some thick hot cider, and a place near their fire. When he had warmed himself, the men could see that his open face and luminous eyes appeared more human and not as the ghostly figure they first saw. Sensing their questions, the boy, pointing past the cliffs, said, "I have been living on a beach. The dolphins put me there, but I don't know where I was before that." All the while, he held a stone tightly in his hand.

"You must have been on a ship that sunk, my boy," said one of the men. The boy, not knowing the answer, just shrugged. The sailors called him Marius, because he came from the sea. They welcomed him into their company for the night and found some spare tattered clothing and a pair of boots on their boats. Slipping the stone safely into his pocket, the young man fell asleep listening to fisherman talk of the elusive schools of flounder and bluefish and cod and the riches held beneath the sea. In the morning Marius was invited aboard the fishing vessel anchored in the cove. He felt a strange pull from the shore as he waded to the boat.

She had not come back. He had not found her when he searched the beach late into the night as the others slept. He scanned the cliffs and sand once again. Finally he put aside the longing he felt and turned instead to go with the men.

Marius made himself useful on the boat, coiling the heavy ropes and casting the nets. The captain was a kind man who had a son named Billy, about the same size as Marius. The captain sent them both to the bow of the ship and told the boys to stand watch for the boiling surface of ocean that signaled the presence of a school of fish. Billy showed Marius where to stand and how to hold on. As they leaned into the wind, they would glance at each other, each curious about the other. Soon they were laughing and wagering about when and where the first fish would appear.

Marius was the one who pointed moments before the school surfaced off to starboard.

Standing at the point of the bow and braced against his friend, Marius closed his eyes. Reaching his hands toward the fish, he called to them in high haunting sounds that only he and the fish could hear. They swam to the boat, some leaping high above the water in their joyous clamor to reach the boy, only to find themselves captured in the nets. The fishermen were overwhelmed by their catch.

Marius's delight in seeing the fish rush toward him turned to horror when he faced the deck and watched each full net dumped into the hold of the ship. As he felt the last struggles of the dying fish, a pain burned deep in his chest. He began to cry great tears that fell into the waves at the side of the boat. He was ashamed of what he had done. But he was also ashamed of his tears, because he was the only one among them who cried.

Marius retreated alone to the stern of the boat and stayed many hours, frightened and confused. At some moments, the water flowing past called to him, and he considered jumping in to return to a time and place that was slipping away. Billy, sensing his new friend's turmoil, came to sit near him. He found no words to help.

Later, when Marius and Billy joined the others gathered about for their evening meal, the men rejoiced at their catch and praised the boy for his work. Marveling at the boy's strange power, they spoke about it, not with the boy, but quietly among themselves. Avoiding the mounded platter of fish in the center of the table, Marius helped himself to boiled potatoes and hard biscuits. But he began to feel that perhaps it was not wrong to help his new friends. That thought lightened the heaviness in his heart.

The next day he reluctantly took his place again with Billy at the bow. When the boys saw a school of fish in the distance, Billy looked at him and waited. Marius hesitated, fists clenched, and then slowly mounted the rail.

Each day for a week the boy called the fish to the nets, and each day the men gave the boy gifts, some silver coins, a leather pouch, and much praise for his work. Marius began to feel proud of his power and challenged himself to do better each day, blocking out the cries of the dying fish.

Although Marius lived on land with the captain and his family, he never quite felt at ease in their spacious home in the midst of a bustling town. He often slept on the beach or at the end of the dock, close to the comfort of the sea. Billy and he remained friends, for Billy had witnessed his deepest sorrow and, without understanding it, had stood fast.

Other young men in the town were not so kind, taunting him as he walked alone through the narrow streets. "Fishboy!" they would call, throwing pieces of bait or rusty hooks at him. They recognized something different about him, and they were jealous that this stranger had won the notice and praise of the most skilled of sea captains.

One evening, while sitting near the shore, a group of the young men approached Marius from behind with a large fish net. Marius sensed their nearness and knew what was about to unfold. He sat motionless while they blindfolded and bound him in the net. He remained silent even as they laughed and shoved and taunted him.

But as they started dragging him toward the water's edge, he began one by one to name their names. With each name, he spoke a hidden truth about that boy, revealing a stolen knife in a pocket, a struggle to read, or a beating taken from a drunken father. The boys stopped and backed away.

Marius, keeping his own fury and fear barely held in his even voice, then asked, "Shall I continue?" The boys, shocked and shamed, slowly moved to loosen their captive. Some stumbled backwards; others turned and ran into the dark. Marius, alone again and weeping, raised his fists and raged at the silent stars and the world around him. He then vowed to weep no more.

The young man, nurtured in the depths of the sea, became a fisherman renowned for his uncanny command of the creatures of that world. His skin browned from hours in the sun, and his muscles thickened from the weight of heavy nets. Soon Marius purchased his boat and found his rewards in the jingle of coins in his pocket, the full larder of his ship's hold, and the endless pursuit of fish. He became accustomed to the respect and awe and even fear of his fellow fishermen, for they only saw the sure and often arrogant face he chose to show them.

He built a cottage on a lonely point of the harbor where the sea all but surrounded him. But Marius began to feel the dulling of the crystal's power beneath layers of sadness that settled on him.

One day as he walked the docks to his ship, he realized he did not understand what the seagulls were saying as they flew overhead. As he watched some children play on the beach, he could not remember his last joyous moment riding to shore on a wave. He could no longer hear the voice of the girl with red hair. With the silence in his heart, there was nothing to check his urge to command the seas and its creatures. Having lost all else, he began to fear that even his power over the fishes would leave him, too.

One morning before dawn after a sleepless night Marius set out alone in his boat with a larder full of provisions. He was followed at a respectful distance by his fellow fishermen, eager to set their nets near him. They sailed for two days on an aimless course as Marius brooded about the direction of his ship, poring over the charts of the unfamiliar waters. The others were confused but had long learned to trust the young man's instincts. What they could not know was that Marius no longer trusted himself and no longer knew which way to go. It was at the end of the third fruitless day, far from their home port, that the young captain finally dropped anchor in the lee of a distant island. Exhausted, he fell into a deep sleep.

Marius didn't know whether what happened next occurred in a dream or a waking place. He found himself upon the bow of the deserted deck as it rocked gently in the blue light of a full moon. He felt a strange peace in the rhythm of the boat—a haunting melody that moved in time with the rising of the bow and a gentle tugging in his chest. He heard a splash and peered over the side to see the heads of five laughing dolphins peering back. Their dance in the waves was so joyful that, before he knew it, Marius had pulled off his clothes and jumped into their midst. They circled him, nudging him playfully with their noses and tails and leaping great distances above his head.

Their giddy reunion lasted hours until at last Marius found himself cradled once again in the pod of dolphins floating in the moonlight. Gently stroking the smooth skins of the animals, he thought of their long years of separation, and the twists and turns of his life since their parting. He began to weep, thinking of the pain he had inflicted on the oceans and its creatures. His loneliness was echoed in the emptiness of the waters around him. The sea had provided enough, but he had taken more.

Reluctantly he returned to his boat. He rubbed each dolphin's head before hauling himself aboard and falling deeply asleep. He was awakened again by their squeaking calls and their bodies thumping against the side of the vessel. The dolphins were warning him of an approaching storm. He signaled to the nearby boats to follow him home, but the other sailors were angry after all the fruitless fishing days and feared he was tricking them again. They refused to follow.

Before the morning sun fully warmed their decks, they saw the dark line of clouds approaching on the horizon.

The storm was fierce. The winds, cold and harsh, bore torrents of biting rain that drenched the fishermen as their vessels bucked through the foaming water. They clung to the masts as each towering wave swept over the deck.

Marius, feeling the power of the storm as he sailed just ahead of it, turned back to help the others. He spotted the dolphins again between the crests of the waves and, with a single sail still hoisted and his hand lashed to the wheel of his vessel, steered toward them. The other sailors, catching a glimpse of his boat, followed as best they could. The bedraggled fleet made their slow and agonizing way through rock-strewn channels to a protected cove.

Marius held steady at the entrance, his arm bruised and cut by the straining ropes, until the last boat passed safely. It was then, as he prepared to follow, that he saw the massive wave—filled with fish and turtles and seaweed and broken bits of boats—all suspended above him, all in the moment before it was to break over his boat. Knowing that his comrades were safe, he loosened his arm from the tiller and surrendered himself to the sea.

Marius drifted loose in the waters, hearing only the sound of his own heart and the muffled waves. He felt the familiar currents of his youth. Among the fishes once again, he glimpsed their wary eyes and darting fins as the waves pushed him farther under. They would not come to him freely now, knowing his power over them and how many had fallen to it.

But he found a peace that he had not known for many years. Even in the depths of the churning sea, he was bathed in a warm light that glimmered off the slow-motion swirl of the sand on the ocean floor. How long he was swept along in the raging riptide that carried him out to sea, he did not know. Only when he felt cold sand against his cheek, the chill air of a crisp night, and glimpsed the stars did he realize he'd been washed ashore on a distant beach.

Seasons

The star child spent many of her days at home watching the change of seasons from the narrow porch or through her little window. The birds came each morning for their bread, but she no longer spoke to them or asked their stories. Often when they fluttered about, she felt a pang in her heart, a nameless longing for something old and lost. She devoted herself to her work and made garments of soft linen and wool embroidered with the fanciful silhouettes of sea creatures and birds.

With the wooden scraps the old man left from his bowls, she constructed birdhouses that she covered with shells and moss she gathered at the water's edge. She hung their fanciful forms on every tree about the cottage. And each week, one of the couple or both of them carried their wares to the village to sell while Terra remained, tending the garden. Having grown into a young woman, she did much of the heavy work that the old man once did.

One market day Terra looked outside her window and saw a young mourning dove perched there with straw in her mouth. The star child watched the busy dove fly back and forth to find twigs for the nest she was building in the corner of the sill.

"Shall I bring you some scraps of wool?" asked Terra. The bird looked up, surprised to hear Terra speaking to her. She blinked and cocked her head and waited as Terra gathered some pieces to help the bird in her work.

Later, when Terra watched the old man trudge down the road toward the village, she noticed the slowness in his steps and remembered the lines of age upon his face. A soft golden glow enveloped him in the early morning light, and he appeared almost transparent. Terra found herself running to catch up with him.

"Let me help you with that sack today," she offered.

He turned to Terra, his eyes soft and suddenly tearful. "You've been a blessing to us, my dear," he said quietly after they continued on.

"We were lucky to find each other," she replied lightly, not wanting to echo the melancholy she heard in his voice. Terra carried his sack until they approached the village bridge, where she stopped. He turned to smile at her, knowing she would not want to go farther. She hugged him tightly and handed over the sack, holding the sight of him until he disappeared from view.

Terra walked home slowly, talking to herself as she often did. "There is something wrong. What is it I fear?" Late in the day she waited in the rocker on the porch, pondering the strange tugging and weight upon her chest and waiting for the old man to return home. When she saw two men approaching slowly leading a horse cart, she called to the old woman. The two women saw their dear one lying in the back of the cart as if asleep. They clung to each other, weeping, when they understood.

In the weeks that followed, Terra and the old woman moved about the cottage carefully, as if there was something fragile and strained that might break. Everywhere was a reminder of the old man—his tools on the shelf, his pipe left on the porch. The old woman, already slow with age and the stiffening of her body, now walked with the burden of her grief. Terra took up the extra chores and did her best to comfort the woman. But Terra could see that the elder's life was seeping away through the wound of her husband's death.

One evening as they ate supper, Terra noticed that the woman was pale and feverish. She prepared some tea and helped the woman into her quilted bed for the night. Instead of climbing to her loft, Terra sat in the chair by the woman's bed as she had her first day on earth. The room was much the same as it had been that spring afternoon. The comb that had been so curious lay on the table. The lace curtains were pulled closed.

The old woman reached for Terra's hand as she struggled to speak. "We only wanted to save you," she whispered, her voice trailing off. Terra, confused, stroked the woman's hand and pondered her words.

Then Terra saw that the woman's eyes were intent upon something in the distance that Terra could not see. She thought she smelled the sweet scent of the tobacco of the old man's pipe. "Thank you, dear one," she spoke, kissing the old woman and then settling herself into the chair for the night.

In the morning she listened to the dove and heard the bird's mate cooing in the distance. She knew by the absence of kitchen sounds and the stillness of the usually creaking floors—and the cold sigh of the wind about the chimney—that the old woman's spirit had passed beyond the bounds of her body.

Terra bade her farewell with tears and songs and buried her next to her husband in the meadow while the mourning doves stood watch. She spoke their names once again, for she was grateful for all they had given her: the songs, the carefree days in the meadow, their protection, and the skill she had learned with the wood tools, the plow, and the needle. All had been gifts passed freely from their hearts.

That evening, the star child watched the dusky pink shadows retreating from the porch and followed them with her eyes across the broad sky to the edge of her world. At first she felt anxious as the darkness approached, and then she dreaded that the sun's return would bring with it the certainty of a lonely day. She knew nothing of the world beyond, only the tender and ragged shape of the empty place she felt within. She had only herself now and only a glimmer of who and what she really was. Sometime in the darkness of that solitary night she accepted that as enough.

The star child rose in the morning and, greeting the nesting doves, welcomed the new sun. She tidied the cottage, prepared a small breakfast, and placed on the table the sack that her dear Papa had carried. Digging through the old trunk that she had not opened in years, Terra found the dress that had been stored there so long ago. She buried her face in its soft shimmer and felt herself as the joyful child in the meadow. Terra wept then for what she had found and the remembrance it brought of what she had lost. Later that morning, she fashioned the dress into a simple scarf that she wore over her other garments, its glimmering colors giving her comfort.

She wrapped some jars of strawberry jam and placed them in the sack along with a few remaining bowls to sell. On her way to the market, Terra waded at the edge of the meadow pond and into the reedy stripe of water connecting it with the ocean.

She came upon a speckled loon who regarded her with a crisp cock of his head and a careful refolding of his wings. The loon told her good morning in their common tongue, the language born by wind and light. She greeted him back and told him, "I am Terra and I am traveling to the market. May I wander in your stream?"

Welcoming her with a graceful sweep of his wing he told her first about his stream, about its tidal rises and falls and the turtles that sun on the rock at the edge. He recounted the seasons when ice had bridged its banks and how red and gold leaves had spun in its current. And all the while the loon had stood watch.

"Thank you for your story," said Terra as she walked on, chuckling softly to herself. Yet she noticed again how natural she felt talking with the loon, and he did not seem to think it odd that she could speak to him. She wondered if she might ever again find a human with whom she could speak without words. She thought of her dear elders, who had loved her but did not seem to notice all the currents that passed between them. Then she thought of the boy from the sea.

When at last she crossed the narrow bridge that led to the village road, she took a deep breath and willed herself to move forward. Remembering what had happened there, her fear settled like a cold stone within her. She could not fathom how to push it aside or let it go. So she traced its shape within her and carried it.

The village was bustling that day but not too busy to notice the beautiful young woman with the fiery red hair carrying the old man's sack. Several folks greeted her shyly, for they had heard rumors of her presence. Turning toward the center of the village, she chanced upon the freckle-faced young man she had healed when he was a boy. He knew her at once.

"It was you, wasn't it? You helped me that day I fell. I saw the sun and then your red hair and then you were gone." She glanced around to see that they were alone, then nodded.

"I knew someone had been with the old ones, but hardly anyone believed me. I'm Nicky," he said, holding out his hand and blushing a bit as she took it and looked into his eyes.

Terra realized with surprise that he felt what she had done those many years ago was something good.

"I must go tell my family you are here," he said excitedly. He was off before Terra could stop him.

Terra walked on to the market so that she could trade the carved bowls in her sack for flour and molasses and salt. Terra noticed that even those who greeted her were careful to step aside to let her pass. The star child, sensing their misgivings, looked away as if not to notice. As she stood at one of the market stalls, the merchant nervously wrapped her provisions and pushed them to her across the table. She heard him whisper to his wife as she turned away, "That's her, isn't it? She's a strange one, I hear. Don't let her look you in the eye."

Terra pretended not to hear but quickly loaded her packages into her sack and walked to the edge of the village, her face taut. Hearing footsteps behind her she turned and saw a young woman carrying a bundle and hurrying toward her. The woman held a crying baby flushed red with a fever and dry cough. The woman beseeched Terra to take the baby in her arms. But the memories of the furrowed brows of the old couple and their fear clouded her heart.

"Please, I must go now," Terra said as she turned toward home.

When she came again upon the loon, he saw the darkness in her look and her sagging shoulders. "Sit and rest and wait," he said gently. And the loon sat with her, silent and still.

She sat a long time by the water's edge. Her thoughts were a jumble of faces and words. At last her restless mind stopped and she felt only the heaviness of her heart and a great void of loneliness. She wept for all the ways she had closed herself away from her world and others, and she wept for those who were afraid to see her as she was, including herself.

Terra knew then that courage was what she needed to be a human being . . . and forgiveness when she could not find that courage in herself. She breathed in deeply, filling her heart with its first sweet glimmer of peace. The star child bowed in thanks to her new understanding, and to the loon who had wept with her. Terra walked back toward the village and to the child awaiting her touch.

Terra began each day anew. The old ones had taught her well, and she honored them in each careful stitch she embroidered and in her first turning of a stack of small wooden bowls. She planted a garden of vegetables, made herb-scented soap, and bartered for the cloth and yarn she needed for her sewing.

Her trips to town were easier now, and she looked forward to chatting with the villagers and selling her wares. The townspeople often brought their ailing children or neighbors to see her. Terra, in learning to trust her own powers to heal, began to sense the healing properties at work in the herbs grown at her doorstep, in the bark of trees, and in the roots of plants. She made salves and poultices and teas to assist her in her work.

She always refused payment for this work, knowing she was but the bearer of the gift. A few villagers remained wary of her, and some even suspected that she meant harm. Terra felt awkward in their presence, but she learned to offer a smile and hand to whomever she encountered in the village.

The seasons fell upon each other, and soon a year had passed since the old couple had died. Terra gathered meadow flowers and laid them upon their graves, remembering again their many kindnesses. She felt their presence in the way the breeze stood still and in the sharp cry of the catbird that came to perch and sing above her head.

That evening when Terra returned from the old ones' graves and finished her work, she took a walk and found herself at the shore. She thought of the boy from the sea. Since the deaths of the old ones, she often thought about the day she spent with him and longed to know what had become of him. She thought she could hear his voice and the way he laughed and the joyful way he ran through the sand and water. She imagined holding his hand again as she walked the path back to the cottage, each speaking to the other without words.

When Terra finished her supper, she pictured him stooped before the fire, setting the kettle for tea. She thought back to the moment when she had watched him sail away from the cove. Then her heart spoke to her, telling her to seek what she had lost. Terra knew what could be found at her hearth, but the wider world was open to her now. She simply chose to go.

Mountain

There were a few things to pack: provisions of biscuits, hard cheeses wrapped in parchment, apples cushioned in scraps of wool, a pen and paper to record her journey, a wool cape to ward off the chill of the autumn evenings or the cold earth that might be her bed. She selected a single wooden bowl on which the old man spent long and happy hours carving a ring of leaves. The old woman's favorite cap, embroidered with delicate meadow flowers, would come, too. Then there was her medicine bag of balms and herbs and vials of tinctures and oils for mending hearts and broken skin and drawing heat from fevered brows. Terra wrapped her scarf around her neck, and set off for the village. Perhaps someone there could tell her about the fishing fleets that worked these shores.

When she entered the main square of the town, she encountered her dear Nicky, who greeted her with his usual adoring smile. She pulled him aside so she could ask him where the big fishing boats were harbored. The young man, surprised by her question, replied, "There is Cler, a port on the other side of the mountain that shelters our village." He pointed upward.

"And how would I travel there?" Terra asked.

Noticing her heavy sack, Nicky began cautiously, "There is an ancient road that leads there by land, but it is a treacherous path along the cliffs. I have heard tales of a witch who lives there. She pushes unsuspecting travelers to their deaths. And the town is full of thieves and bandits. It would not be safe for you."

Terra listened to his warnings and felt his concern. But she did not feel fear, only a steady pull to walk the mountain path. Finally she told Nicky, "Thank you, Nicky. I will take special care on my journey, and I will watch out for that witch. Don't worry. I'll be back."

Stopping to pay respect to the path that lay before her, Terra opened her heart and mind to what she might find. Silently, she asked permission of the mountain to travel there. She kept a steady pace, alert to every sound and sight. She noticed the wildflowers that dotted the edge of the trail, the leaves that were beginning to turn, the jutting rocks and glimpses of animals that raced ahead to disappear into the low-lying brush. She walked until dark, only stopping for a brief rest and to pick some berries.

She had never slept away from the cottage and nervously began to think where she might settle in the darkness. Remembering her nights among the vegetables in the garden, Terra slowly surveyed the landscape until she saw a large tree. It seemed to beckon to her, and when she crawled into the shelter of its gnarled roots, she felt it wrap her in its bark and leaves. She dreamed that she, too, was a tree, her hands budding like a spring branch, her arms swaying, a nest of birds at the crook of her neck, her feet rooted in the dirt.

As morning came she touched the tree tenderly as she said, "Thank you and farewell." She set out at a brisk pace, hoping to reach the summit by nightfall. As she climbed, the air became cool and crisp. Late in the day Terra found herself engulfed by an icy fog that coated the tender twigs of the surrounding trees and brush. Terra felt the strain of the steady climb, but she also felt a surge of energy beneath her feet as if the road itself was pushing her upward. The path crunched under each step, and she could barely make out its edges through the ghostly cloud that had descended around her.

Exhausted, she stopped for a moment in the middle of the road. Lifting her eyes from the treacherous path, she saw through the ice and fog the still beauty of a mountainside painted with silver light. The road plunged swiftly to the sea on her left, and she could hear the sounds of the surf far below. To her right were huge boulders covered in mosses and surrounded by brush. Directly above her head she saw the filmy face of the moon. Terra sighed and breathed deeply of the cold air. Momentarily refreshed, she smiled.

Terra started to push on and to look for another night shelter. She began to feel a tingling in her spine and neck, the unseen presence of another. Just then she saw a movement on the road ahead. She hugged her cloak about her shoulders, fingering the scarf that hid beneath it. She wondered if the shadows and the fog and the moonlight could be playing a trick on her. But as she stood still and watched, a dark figure moved closer.

Terra quickly slipped behind a boulder, hoping to disappear into the landscape. At last the being, shrouded in dark shawls and bent over a walking stick, came close and stopped. Terra held her breath until she heard the shuffling footsteps continue past.

It's the witch, thought Terra. Listening to every step grow fainter, Terra waited until the only sound was the ocean. She stood up and peered about. Seeing nothing, she stepped upon the road and began a quick walk, stopping occasionally to listen and glance backward. As she rounded the next turn in the road she stopped short, her hand going to her mouth to hold back a scream. The figure now stood directly in her path.

"Who travels here?" demanded the voice of an old woman.

Terra could not speak.

"I asked, 'Who travels here?'"

"I am Terra. I wish to cross this mountain road."

"So you think I am behind you, eh?"

Terra, sensing her folly and feeling there was no escape, replied cautiously. "You seem to be everywhere I turn."

"Ah, yes." The woman waited, then asked, "Then why is it that you hide yourself from me?"

Terra quickly blurted out, "I was told you were a dangerous . . . witch," her voice trailing off.

"Is that so? And what do *you* tell yourself?"

"I don't know if you are a witch, or dangerous. But I am afraid."

The old woman lifted her head to consider the young woman standing before her. "And if you were not afraid, what *then* would you see?"

Terra dug deep within for an answer, trying to part the heavy mantle of fear that weighted her. Finally she spoke in a soft but clear voice, "You are not dangerous, though I suspect you have powers that may be frightening to many . . . and to me."

"I see," the old one replied. "And so you hid because you were afraid to see the truth. And because you were unable to see the truth, you were afraid?" Terra nodded.

"And why have you come to this place, my dear?"

Terra answered simply, "I am on a journey to find someone I lost long ago. I don't know where it will take me. I have lost my own way many times."

"Finding ourselves is the only journey that matters, my dear." With this, the woman nodded and turned, gesturing for Terra to follow. As they moved through the fog, Terra felt a deep calm.

The cave where the woman led her was perched high above the road in the face of the mountain. Its opening was obscured by the rocks strewn about and was invisible from both the shore and the road. Inside a fire smoldered, and the woman pointed for Terra to sit and warm herself. Terra hesitated briefly, her eyes darting about the space.

The elderly woman shuffled about, setting her hooded cloak aside. Terra saw her wrinkled face and bony fingers. Gazing into her warm and sad eyes, Terra could see there was kindness there, and she felt less afraid. A trio of animals gathered around them. A brown rabbit nuzzled Terra's feet; far from its home in the marshes, a dragonfly rested on the woman's shoulder; and a great owl blinked from its perch on the rock behind the old woman.

Terra and the woman shared a pot of tea and sat quietly without speaking. At last the woman said, "I am called the Ancient Mother. I have been waiting for you to come since I first saw the star that landed in the meadow. You have learned much." Pausing to look again at Terra, she went on, "You chose to come here to learn something about being a human. That is the task for everyone here on earth, but we sometimes forget where we came from and what we already know."

Terra closed her eyes, remembering the ways this had been true in her life. As the Ancient Mother continued, she seemed to read Terra's thoughts. "Others will not always appreciate you and may be afraid of you. But you can appreciate yourself. A human being who knows herself has great power. She can use that for the good of others. Always surrender to your heart, your guide, even if others don't understand."

Grateful for the woman's wisdom, Terra then asked, "Why is it that you do not live in the village? Why are they afraid of you?"

The Ancient Mother, her face lit by the fire, began her story in a soft, steady voice. "Many years ago before your star settled in the meadow, I lived happily in the village with my husband. We worked very hard, I weaving cloth and he as a boatbuilder at the shore. One day a man came to the village looking for laborers to sail with him to build a great trading ship in the town you are now seeking. My husband decided to join the group. I begged him not to leave with the others.

"That night, I fell into a deep sleep and dreamed I was a hawk, flying high above the shore and cliffs. I was hunting for my mate, gliding on powerful wings that caught the currents of air. I cocked my head and saw his ship dashed to pieces against the rocks, and I swooped down in a dead fall. My screams awakened my husband and other villagers, and I tried to tell them what I saw. But I was hysterical and babbling, not knowing if I was bird or woman. They mocked me and told me I was crazy and selfish to carry on like that. My husband left me with the villagers who tied my waving arms and quieted my screams. When the ship sank, the villagers came after me, saying I was a witch and had used my power to curse the ship. They drove me from the town with stones and fire. I have lived alone, high on this mountain, ever since."

The Ancient Mother paused again, the firelight in her eyes reflecting the great sadness of that time. "Your elder ones, they saw what the villagers had done to me. They tried, but they could not save me." The Ancient Mother paused then and looked up at the star child. "The woman who raised you as her own was my daughter." As the weight of those words fell upon Terra, she understood the terror and grief of the old couple and why they had tried to protect her.

After another long silence, the woman continued her story. "I could no longer do my work or be with my family, and it was many years before I learned to forgive the villagers. Forgiveness takes time, and for me, it grew only a little each day.

"Now I light the paths of travelers, keeping them from falling from the cliff. My lanterns have saved many ships from those rocks below. Yet others, in their fear, never look up to see what help is there for them. Only those who stop and wait in stillness will see my light."

Reaching over to touch the place where the crystal was held in Terra's chest, the Ancient Mother continued, "Everyone has what you have, my dear, though perhaps not formed in a crystal. But each cell, each breath has that spark, the memory of the universe and where we came from. If we stand still and surrender to what we cannot know with just our minds, we become like prisms, each of us reflecting the life and light of the universe in our own way. Then we can fulfill our individual destinies. For it is not our minds that tell us our purpose, it is our hearts.

"Not everyone can know the future or see into the minds of others, but all of us can know ourselves, what hurts us and makes us laugh. We must always honor what we feel and respect what we cannot know."

As the Ancient Mother's touch and the truth of her words spiraled into Terra's heart, she felt the presence of her dear elder ones. A deep understanding and forgiveness settled within her. Terra bowed in respect to the old woman and, wrapping herself into her cloak, soon fell into a deep, safe sleep.

As the sun's rays crept across the wall of the cave, Terra awakened to see the silhouette of the woman sitting at the entrance, her face to the rising sun. The woman's arms moved outward to welcome the day as her body rocked gently, chanting a song to the light. Terra waited until the woman stood and turned, and she thought she saw for a moment, instead of the craggy lines of the old woman's face, the features of a young woman smiling at her.

Terra began to gather her things for the rest of her journey. The woman gave her some water and walked back into the cave to retrieve a willow staff. She stood before Terra and handed her the gift. "Willow is a wise wood, strong because it can bend. Carry this with you and learn what it may teach. While we journey on earth, we must learn to be a part of earth. For our spirits are meant to know the beauty that we sense with the bodies we have been given and the harmony that is taught by the animals and plants, sea and sky."

Terra hugged the old woman and, thanking her for her help, kissed her gently on the cheek. As Terra turned to leave, the woman said, "There is another like you, my child." Terra's heart leaped at these words, and she saw the face of the boy from the beach. The woman reached up and touched her forehead. Then Terra saw the face of a man, lying cold and wet on a windswept shore. Her breath shortened. Terra wished to ask more, but the Ancient Mother had shown her what she would. With her staff in hand, Terra turned to the narrow path that led to the mountain road.

Awakening

arius, feeling the surf about his feet and the bright sun drying his body and tattered clothes, rested a moment more upon the sand, lost in the dreams of swirling waters that had brought him to shore. Coughing seawater from his throat and feeling the battering that the waves and rocks had left upon his body, he was grateful that he had survived. He remembered the wave that had washed him from his ship and from his life. Marius knew he never again wished to see fear in the eyes of the creatures of the sea or any living thing. He slowly rose from the sand.

Marius was startled to see the familiar shape of the sea rock where the dolphins had first left him. His thoughts turned quickly to the girl he had met there, her red hair bright in the sun and the soft feel of her hand in his.

He started off in the direction of the tidal stream that wound first through the dunes and then on to the meadow hills beyond. He came upon the loon perched upon a fallen log, and they regarded each other with a nod. The loon immediately recounted the entire story of his stream, the dizzying dance of the leaves in the current, the turtles that sun on the rocks, and the never-ending cycle of tides. He finished his tale with a careful preening of a wing feather and then inspected the man who sat patiently before him.

Marius told the loon how he had survived the wreck of his ship. When finished, he asked, "Where might I find some food and lodging?" Pointing with an outstretched expanse of wing, the loon directed him toward the village. Just before turning to leave, Marius thought again of the nameless girl whose young face sprang to his mind.

"What you seek is very close," replied the loon instantly, his words fueling a tender new hope in Marius.

Marius walked on to the village. His bedraggled look and sand-specked hair and clothing were a curiosity to the villagers who showed him to the well and drew him some water. After resting, Marius wandered the narrow streets and found himself near the open door of a baker's shop, drawn there by the welcoming aromas.

The old baker, his brow wet and flushed from the heat of the blazing oven, turned to see who had come to buy bread. Marius seemed at once familiar. Marius also felt comfortable here in this small room and in the presence of the older man. They stared at one another for a moment until the baker's dog entered and raced across to the young man, almost knocking him over with his paws on his chest and his muzzle in his face.

"Whoa there," said the baker, as he reached for the usually diffident hound. "I think he likes you," he said, chuckling.

Before long, the baker and Marius found themselves in a long conversation over hot soup and bread. Marius, famished from his ordeal, welcomed the warm meal and a place to rest. He told the baker about the storm and shipwreck and then fell silent as he felt the weight of his life as a fisherman.

"I am not certain about what I shall do now, but I am grateful to be alive," Marius said. The baker gazed at his visitor and sensed that he had much in common with the young man. He told Marius his story:

"I came to this village from a farm many miles from here, seeking my fortune, full of myself and sure that I would conquer the world. I was big and quick-tempered and sought to prove myself in the world of men. I found work shearing sheep in the spring and harvesting crops in the summer and fall. I was known for my fighting skill, and no man dared to challenge me. But I did not know how to have power over myself. I became very lonely and trusted no one. In looking after only myself, I forgot to see that others were human like me. I forgot to be kind.

"One day as I walked through the street with a band of men, a beggar approached me for bread. I kicked him out of my way in a fit of rage. I laughed as I saw his body roll over in the dust. The beggar simply looked back at me, and I'll never forget his eyes. He stared into me without fear. I was the one afraid and hungry. He was the one who was fearless and giving. I reached for his hand and lifted him up from the dirt.

"Something changed in me then. I no longer had the will to fight and hurt others. Once I had seen myself, I could not pretend to be someone else. But I didn't know how to live otherwise, and I spent many days feeling helpless and unable to work. My sister took me in, and some days I would sit in her kitchen oblivious to everything. Then I began to watch her bake bread. I began helping her and learned to make loaves myself. I saved my money and built this place. I will always have bread for the beggars, for I know now that it is they who are giving to me when I feed them."

Marius heard the truth in the words of the man, and he wanted to learn more from him. The baker, sensing the goodness of the lost seaman, invited Marius to stay and learn his trade.

The old baker was a good teacher and grateful for the helper who had found his way to his door. The lessons he shared were not simply in the technique of baking. Marius was instructed to spend long hours simply observing the fire in the great stone oven. He learned how the fierce energy of the flames would spend itself to create an even heat for baking. He watched carefully as the baker opened vents to feed the fire and bank the coals against the walls of the oven. Sometimes he lost himself in daydreams as he gazed at the glowing embers and licking flames.

Other days he meticulously whisked every speck of flour and crumb from the storage bins and shelves. The pans and utensils were washed and dried carefully after each use and placed in their own special spot to be found again the next day. Marius learned to not be wasteful of anything and took care with his tools. The old baker taught him to offer a blessing before he began his work and when he finished for the day. His apprenticeship moved on to mixing and handling the dough. He learned the aromas of the different flours, the rye and wheat and corn, and how their textures felt. He knew from the smell of the kitchen the moment when the bread was fully baked and before the browning crust was burned.

Marius slept on a narrow cot at the rear of the bakery. He was the first to rise in the morning to stoke the ovens. He found he was well suited for the rhythm of this work, easily moving bags laden with flour and taking pleasure in the feel of the dough as he kneaded and shaped the loaves. It became second nature to him to know when the yeast had worked enough and when the fire would receive the bread and yield it back to him crisp and hot. He felt, for the first time, joy in the work of his hands.

When the loaves finished cooling on the wooden racks, he wrapped the best to carry to the poorer families who lived in shacks at the edge of the village. He'd stop to play with the children and show them magic tricks. He dropped crumbs for the birds and mice that gathered at the rear courtyard. The rest of the bread was sold or traded for vegetables and eggs and cheese from the villagers who brought with their offerings news of the countryside.

It wasn't long before Marius began to work with those offerings and created luscious fruit and savory pies. The aromas of cherry or apple or melting cheeses drew even more to the shop. And the bakers found that the more they gave away, the more they seemed to have to sell.

Marius thrived in his new life in the village. His ready smile and listening ear made him many friends and always welcome at village gatherings. He sometimes took long walks along the shore at dusk, finding great comfort in the sound of the sea and the feel of saltwater against his skin. He often stopped by the loon's stream to chat with him. At the end of the day, the ancient sea rock once again became his perch as he watched the sun dip into the darkening sky. At these times Marius thought of the girl.

One evening while he wandered the shore he found an overgrown path leading up toward a meadow. He followed it through blackberry hedges and came upon an empty cabin, the porch unswept and the door pulled tight. He was drawn to the place and found himself sitting upon the porch when he noticed the birdhouses covered in shells that dotted the trees. He knew suddenly that this was the home of the girl.

Marius hurried back to the village to talk with the baker. He was sitting at the kitchen table sharpening knives when Marius burst into the room. The baker chuckled to himself when he saw the flushed face of his friend. "Tell me about the red-haired girl who lived in the cottage with the birdhouses."

"Have you seen her? Do you know her?" the baker replied, surprised at Marius's sudden interest. "She hasn't been here in many months, since before you arrived in the village."

Marius sat down in disappointment but pressed the man for more information. "I met her long ago. But who is she? Where did she go?"

The baker shrugged. "No one seems to know where she is. She arrived here mysteriously many years ago and lived with an old couple outside town. We rarely saw her. Then, one day after the old couple died, she started coming to town. And now she seems to have just as mysteriously disappeared.

"She was a hard worker, helping the old ones and then growing that garden herself. She seemed to have a certain touch in helping folks who were sick. I heard stories."

Marius only knew that he wanted to find her.

Just then, Nicky appeared at the door. "Ah, here's just who we need to talk to. Come have a seat and some pie," said the baker. As the young man dug into the dish set before him, the baker asked him about Terra.

He stopped chewing and his whole body slumped. Nicky raised his head slowly and finally stammered out, "Terra's gone over the mountain. I warned her not to go. I told her about the witch. I don't know where she is or if she is ever coming back." He looked away, the burden of his secret shared and his fear and sadness seeping out.

Marius took it all in. "Terra. Terra," he said again and again to himself, as if repeating her name could make her appear.

Hope

On another day and in another place, Terra walked toward Cler, aided by the willow staff and the new openness she felt. The Ancient Mother had touched her heart, and she moved with a sureness in her step. Thinking of the boy from the sea, she knew that he had grown to manhood. Her vision of him on the mountain told her that he had endured many trials since their parting.

Finally she glimpsed the sea town from a small hilltop. Cler bustled with commerce, the women minding small children and baskets of produce in the center of the market. She could see the fishermen on the loading docks returning from their expeditions.

Terra slipped into town among the other visitors looking for provisions and shelter. She found her way through the narrow streets to the harbor full of fish vendors drying their nets and buyers haggling over prices. She walked along the docks, peering into the vessels, studying the faces of the men who worked on the decks. For the first time, Terra realized she did not know the name of the man she sought. Until now, his memory, held tenderly in the spaces of her heart, had been enough.

Terra bought fresh fruit and bread in the market and sat on an old crate as she ate and watched children chasing one another under the market tables and around the stalls. She liked the bustle of the market and realized that the warnings given by her friend about bandits were only his effort to keep her from leaving. She would find a place to sleep and decide in the morning what she might do next.

She wandered the streets away from the main dockside inns and shops until she came to a sign advertising a room to let. Stepping inside, she found a young woman preparing the evening meal.

"I'm Brigit," she said as Terra peered inward. "Come in, come in."

Her ready smile made Terra feel welcome, and Terra paid a few coins to sleep in the cozy room just off the kitchen. A toddler crawled about the floor, a fire burned in the hearth, and a huge pot of soup simmered above the flames. Terra offered to help with a basket of mending she saw next to the large wooden table in the middle of the room. She sat in the window seat and began repairing woolen shirts snagged by fishing hooks and tiny socks worn by the three children of the house.

Before long the whole family gathered for dinner. Each of them, from the oldest son to the husband, Billy, whose heavy step was marred by a limp, greeted Terra with a nod and quiet hello. They gathered about the table, sharing their stories of the day. When at last the family turned to Terra, she told them of her journey over the mountain and that she was seeking a young man whom she had not seen for many years.

For the first time, she shared the story of her meeting with the boy. Abandoning her shyness, she began to describe his features, hoping someone might know about him. "His hair was brown and wavy. He had green eyes. He wore a necklace made of shells and sea glass."

Billy, suddenly startled by the picture she had portrayed of the boy, turned pale. "Marius!" he whispered and dropped his head into his hands. The others stopped their chatter and the room became silent. Terra held her breath and waited for the man to speak.

"My father found Marius wandering the shore on the other side of the island many years ago. I sailed with him on that first voyage, and we became friends. Father brought him to live with us, and we shared a room and played on the docks together. He became a fisherman, like me, and he was so good at finding the fish that he soon had his own boat and moved to his own house at the edge of the harbor. In those last years, he kept to himself a lot, but I always will love him as my brother."

The man paused for a moment and Terra waited, sensing there was more not yet told. His voice slowed as he struggled to tell the story of that last sail far from port, the sudden storm, how Marius led the others to safety, and the mammoth wave he saw crash over Marius's boat. "It was just over a year ago that we lost him," he said quietly, his eyes filled with tears as he stood and looked off toward the sea.

Terra leaned back against her chair, trying to make the words into some sense while her mind grasped for any truth other than what she heard. Struggling with her own grief, she reached to touch Billy's arm. As his family slowly gathered to stand about him, Terra slipped away to her room.

Terra stood numbly by her window and stared across the rooftops toward the harbor. Even her vision on the mountain had not prepared her for this blow, and now every part of her fought against it. Exhausted, she crumpled into her bed and cried until she fell into a deep sleep. In her dream that night she wandered the shore alone, far from home, seeking stones worn into the shape of hearts. She filled her pockets with them, but something urged her to hunt for more. She finally stopped; looking out to sea, she saw five dolphins watching her. They had been swimming unnoticed alongside her on her long trek. They sang out to her, "Rest. What you seek will find you."

When Terra awoke the next morning she asked the fisherman if he would show her the place where Marius had lived. On their walk, Billy told Terra about Marius's life with them—stories of his card-playing prowess, his abilities to sense without seeing, and his command of the seas and fish.

Billy could not bring himself to go inside Marius's house and stood watching the waves as he waited for Terra. Terra stopped at the door and silently asked the house if she could enter. She moved slowly through the rooms, each with a window opening to the sea. She closed her eyes and wandered farther until she found herself back by the empty hearth. Beside it sat a leather chair and a small table holding a carved wooden box. Terra opened the box and saw the heart-shaped stone. She held it to her, and in the soft pulse that moved through her hand, she knew that Marius was still alive.

Terra walked the steps from the house to the gate in silence. As she and the fisherman resumed their walk, she asked if she might stay with them longer until she decided what to do next.

"Marius is still alive," she said softly.

He stopped, then looked at her, and replied, "I have wished it so against all hope. I pray you are right, dear lady. But I cannot break open this wound that has only just begun to heal."

In the following months Terra helped the family with their chores, finished the mending in the basket, and fashioned new garments for the children. She liked being part of a family again and welcomed her talks with Brigit as they trudged to the market or made meals or bathed the children.

Terra began to share her healing talents with the family, mixing salves for bee stings and cuts and teas for scratchy throats. One evening, as the fisherman pulled off his heavy boots to dry by the fire, she asked if she might see his injured foot. "It was the spiny fin of a fish that caught me last spring. It has never healed right." She examined his wounded foot, still red and swollen around the point of puncture. She mixed her herbs and placed a paste on the wound, holding her hands above the place until he felt the wound grow warm. In three days the foot was healed without a trace of injury.

Terra often walked to the harbor to watch the visiting ships make their way through the channel, hoping that one would carry Marius. But after many months, when the days began to lengthen and grow warmer, Terra's thoughts returned to her cottage. The doves would begin their nesting soon, and it was time to plant her herbs and vegetables. She knew it was time to go home.

"Terra, dear, you are so quiet today. Shall we walk out by the water a bit and get a little air?" Brigit's round face, framed in dark curls, looked at her expectantly. Terra agreed, and they strolled on the sand until they sat upon a large driftwood log. Watching the water and the parade of white clouds gliding above them, Terra spoke at last.

"I thought that I would find him and that he would bring back something I had lost," Terra finally said, tracing circles in the sand with her toes.

"You are lucky, Brigit. You know your place and have a companion who shares your life. I have always felt separate and alone." Seeing Brigit's expression she hastened to add, "Oh, not that I don't feel your love. You are like a sister to me. It's just that I know that I came from somewhere else and haven't always felt that I belong here."

"We have all felt Marius's loss, dear Terra. It is a sharing, however painful, that makes you a part of us," responded Brigit, as she reached for Terra's hand.

Terra, looking at her friend, admitted, "I am of two worlds and am just beginning to put them together. I thought maybe that finding Marius, seeing me in him, would make me whole. But I know now that only I can do that . . . and I must and I can. I have everything I need."

Then Terra laughed and, hugging her friend, said, "I guess I am like that big pot of yours on the hearth. I must tend to it, gathering and stirring *all* the pieces of myself. I'll let it simmer and make of me what it will."

"But Terra," Brigit teased, "don't forget to add a little spice." Terra laughed as they rose and brushed off the sand and walked back arm in arm.

Terra told the family that night that she was ready to begin her walk to her own home. The next morning she was given food to carry with her and Brigit's reassuring but tearful smile. Terra told the family how they might find her and promised to return after the fall harvest.

Faith

The journey homeward was bittersweet for the star child. She looked forward to the quiet familiarity of the village and the warmth of her own cottage by the sea. Her thoughts of Marius were surprisingly strong, having walked the places he walked and known and touched the people who had been part of his life. But she did not dwell on his absence.

Terra carried gifts for the Ancient Mother—food and a woolen shawl Terra had knitted. She at last arrived at the narrow path leading to the cave. The old woman sat waiting, and Terra rushed forward to greet her.

"My child, it is good to be with you again. I see that your heart stays open and strong. Come," said the Ancient Mother. Terra followed her into the cozy warmth and settled in for the evening. She recounted stories of her life in Cler and what she had learned there about Marius. "I know he is still alive, but I also know I may never see him again," Terra said quietly, waiting for the Ancient Mother to respond.

"Then trust your heart, my dear," she said simply. After a few moments she continued, "We must not live our lives as if they are to be another way.

We can only live each moment deeply, fully, and with acceptance. Then we know that we are truly living and fulfilling our purpose here. Only then can we be open to the gifts that we receive every day. For many years after I came here, I held on to regret and fantasy. I'd think, 'If only my husband were still here,' or, 'If only I could go home.' When I stopped thinking that way, I began to notice how beautiful this place was and how much I loved the solitude of the mountain air. The animals came to me and accepted me. And now, today, this moment, I have you. My life is good."

Terra and the Ancient Mother watched the fire for a long time before the Elder spoke again: "I will not talk of whether you will find Marius, for even if you do, you must always know that there is nothing permanent in this physical world. Only the love you give yourself and others is eternal. Whatever happens, welcome your happiness, welcome your grief, welcome each person that you meet. They are all your teachers." The two women gazed at each other as Terra thanked her for her wisdom.

In the morning, Terra took leave once again of the Ancient Mother. Before she left, Terra wrapped the beautiful shawl around the old woman. The iridescent threads running through the white wool sparkled when they captured the rays of the early sun. Terra hugged the Ancient Mother, took up her staff, and felt a great sense of anticipation as she stepped onto the path.

As the evening light ebbed she sought a shelter for the night. She noticed a small opening in the thicket that lined the road and walked into the darkening forest. She found herself in a clearing surrounded by towering white birches. As she approached, the sounds of the forest seemed to hush, and she stopped to bow before entering the circle of trees.

She stood watching in wonder as golden threads of dusky air lit the forest floor. Feeling waves of energy rising through her feet and into her arm, the star child raised the willow staff. At each place she pointed the staff the earth responded. The sound of leaves in the breeze became a melody. The color of the wild iris blossom pulsed and burst forth in a sprinkling of purple stars. A deer paused to watch Terra from deep, brown-eyed pools. She knew all was already set in motion. Yet it was in her power to use what had been given her to touch the world around her and let the world touch her. In that moment, Terra saw and called forth the soul that lay beneath.

She stayed in her magical forest until the stars, whispering her name, called her to a dream place where even their bright light faded into a deep blackness. She floated in the rhythmic motion of the great Cosmic Breath. And she was All and No More.

After hearing Nicky's story of Terra's journey, Marius was both dazed and excited by the prospect that he might find Terra, even though he did not fully understand the depth of his feelings. Perhaps it was because she was the first human contact he had found in his solitary life on the beach. Perhaps it was her enchanting beauty or the suddenness with which he had found and then lost her. His mind could conjure the reasons, but it was the sweetness and longing in his heart, like the feel of the heart-shaped stone he had carried with him all those years, that defied explanation. He wanted to immediately go and search for her. At the same time he chided himself for his impatience.

He fretted about returning to his old home in Cler, for he held many regrets about how he had lived his life there: lonely, arrogant, and enamored with his own skill. That night he dreamed he was clinging to the side of a mountain, inching closer to the top. Below, steep rocks and crevices fell away to the valley from which he had climbed. Above, the precipice jutted outward, a seemingly impossible climb to the summit. He was not sure if he had the strength and skill to climb over the edge to safety. He knew he might not survive the fall and wished he had never set out on the climb. He was pondering his choices, his exhausted body facing the craggy rock wall, when he awakened breathless and with his heart pounding.

That morning as they worked side by side, the baker sensed his helper's agitated state and placed his hand on his shoulder. Marius told him his dream. The baker smiled as he gazed into the young man's troubled face. "Like that mountain, we cling to our world, our beliefs, our illusions, because it is how we have learned to survive in this world. It is all we know. It is only when we let go that we learn that we also have wings. In a world we summon by faith, we find we can fly."

The kindly baker paused, then continued, "You are remembering how your gifts were not tempered by love and how much you gave up to please others. But you have learned great lessons from that time, from the pain that you endured. You have learned about yourself. Have faith in that."

Marius thought over these words, then asked, "But what if I forget? I don't ever want to be like that again."

"But part of you is always that lonely young man, that arrogant fisherman. The ways you used to survive are still within you. Make friends with those parts, too. Find the strength that is there.

"Marius, when your heart tells you that it is right, then you must obey and find a way to search for her. Meanwhile I will ask Nicky to help me while you are away." Marius, his heart full of hope, thanked the baker and pondered his words as he shaped the loaves.

Marius made preparations for his departure by stocking up and storing extra bags of flour. He began coaching Nicky, teaching him what he had been taught. He felt a new lightness, and he whistled as he carried his treasures to his friends and spent extra time with the children there in games of chase or chance.

Many evenings Marius would make his way back to the shore and the cottage in the meadow. He would sometimes just sit on the porch in the rocker or pull weeds from the hedge. He repaired the creaking wooden gate to the kitchen garden and mended the rabbit fence. He noticed the many herbs growing about and would stop to smell their fragrance. He watched pairs of birds lay claim to their homes and heard their songs, bright and hopeful.

He never entered the cottage, but peeked through the window at times, the humble furnishings expectant and inviting. He mapped their place in his mind, hoping for the day he would see a pair of boots at the door, some flowers in the vase on the table, a curtain slipping through an open window, any sign that Terra had returned.

One evening, Marius nodded off on the porch under the spell of a sweet spring breeze. He awoke with a start and, gazing upward, saw the flash of white wings and the shadow of a hawk against the bright face of the full moon. He knew in an instant that he must begin his journey. He headed home to the bakery and quickly made his final preparations to leave. He bade farewell to Nicky and the baker, and they watched his joyful step on the path that led to the edge of the village. Eager and excited, there also grew in him a sure and quiet resolve. Marius knew he could trust his heart to show him the way.

Joy

*H*aving walked steadily through the night, Marius paused to rest and eat. From his perch at the side of the road, he noticed a parting of the shrubs that led into the forest. He was drawn inward, suddenly alert to every sound and movement around him. At the clearing ahead, surrounded by white birches, he saw her. Red hair streamed down her back as she sat facing the center of the circle. Then she stood and slowly turned to face him.

Transfixed, Marius stood for long moments. He felt neither the ground nor the movement of his own legs as he finally stepped forward.

He saw the beauty of her pale skin and clear blue eyes and the sorrow and joys that she had known etched upon her brow and in the soft curve of her shoulders. Terra was drawn to the deep green eyes that looked like the ocean.

In that moment, memories rushed through them, drawn deep from beyond the bounds of their earthly home. They had been part of one: fragments of the same massive sun that had tossed fiery pieces of rock into the farthest reaches of the great blackness. And just as that power had flung them apart, so that power now drew them clearly and inevitably to one another.

65

They reached for each other's hands. Terra pulled the scarf from beneath her cloak showing him the same light-filled fabric he had himself worn so long ago. As she touched it to his hand, he marveled at the familiar feel of it and then at the leaping of his heart.

Terra spoke first. "Marius, forgive me that I could not speak the truth that day we met—that you and I had come from the same place. I saw in you what I had been and given up. I saw how you would be hurt by trying to live as a human. I wanted to save you, but I didn't even know how to save myself. It was a path that only brought more of what I hoped to avoid."

Marius nodded. "There is nothing for me to forgive, dear Terra. It seems we both have learned why the earth is bathed in tears. But I know now we have a choice. And now I remember the joy."

Terra reached her hand to his face. Marius, leaning forward, did the same so that their foreheads touched as they stood in the bright morning sun. If earth and heaven have ever met it was there, a flower rising from the forest floor, perfumed and white and ever unfolding.

They sat then in the clearing, their thoughts and words like a clear stream winding between them. They told stories, laughing about the loon, and sharing news of Cler and the village, the baker and the Ancient Mother. And at times they sat unspeaking, as they once did so long ago on the sea rock, basking in the warmth of each other's presence and the sun moving across the sky.

The pair talked late into the night by the moon's glow. Gazing again into Terra's eyes, Marius kissed her tenderly. "I would like us to go see the Ancient Mother."

"Yes, and to ask her to bless our journey together," replied Terra, speaking what they already knew, pledging themselves to each other.

Terra and Marius traced the rocky road back to the summit. The Ancient Mother awaited them at the mouth of the cave and received them into her open arms. Marius took a deep bow and offered the Ancient Mother a loaf of his bread and a small crock of honey as they waited for her to speak.

"I have prepared a welcome for you," she said.

She led them to a stone slab supported by two small boulders resting on a bluff overlooking the sea. Upon the table—which was covered with green mosses and spring flowers and upright tree branches full of blossoms—sat three stone cups, a bowl of walnuts, dried figs, cheeses, and a salad of mint and violets. She placed the loaf and honey there. The three sat on the ground around the low table, gave thanks, and feasted. The bright sun and the spring air were intoxicating, and only the distant waves and the wind punctuated their nearly silent communion.

As the meal drew to the end, Marius reached across the table for Terra's hand and spoke. "We have promised ourselves to one another, dear Elder. I hope you will bless our journey now together as you have blessed Terra's life before."

The Ancient Mother answered, "Marius, you have received the gift of this meal and you have given many gifts to others. Can you now also receive the gift of yourself?"

Closing his eyes, Marius felt a wave of gratitude filling his heart and coursing through him. His whole being felt vibrant and full of light. He answered clearly, "Yes, I can."

"Ah, yes. Remember, Marius, that what you now feel inside is more powerful than your struggles, greater than your failures, and more beautiful than any part of this earth."

Turning to Terra, the Ancient Mother asked, "Did you hear that?"

Terra smiled and nodded, knowing her words to Marius were meant for her as well.

"Then we have much to bless and celebrate," said the Elder.

The Ancient Mother stood and walked to the edge of the cliff and turned, her silhouette against the sun-dazzled sea. She motioned for Terra and Marius to kneel before her.

She wrapped the white shawl that Terra had given her around both their shoulders and around their hands, joining them together, and spoke. "You ask my blessing on your journey, and that I bestow upon you now." The Ancient Mother raised her hand and blessed a bowl of water that sat before them and handed it to them to share.

"But remember that it is what you carry in your heart and do with your hands and speak with your voices each day that will bless your lives together. May each action be guided by wisdom and by love, for the person that you are meant to be, and for your partner who will help you learn who you really are."

As Terra and Marius looked at each other, the old woman chanted ancient words that touched their hearts and set the crystals vibrating within their chests so that they were enveloped in the sound and each other. And they knew that the love they felt had no limit except that which they chose to trace around it.

The three moved inside the cave as a late-afternoon mist was soon overtaken by roiling clouds and brilliant blue streaks of lightning and the boom of thunder shaking the rocks and their bones. They huddled close, listening to the distant thunder and sharing stories as they waited for the rain.

As evening fell, the Ancient Mother bade them goodnight and retired to her simple pallet at the rear of the cave. Terra and Marius stepped outside, where the rain had left the night air fresh and sweet. Terra leaned against his body as they watched the lightning flash upon the distant sea and sky and an occasional star twinkling through the clouds. In that moment and place, all moments and places were lost to them. They became everything and nothing, boundless and contained. Each sense heightened and connected. The sound of the surf became his heartbeat. The scent of the rain-washed earth became a part of her breath and then the color of roses rushing across her cheeks. Terra and Marius turned to look at each other. Then they, the children of the stars, each saw before them another universe to explore.

Fire

In the morning Terra and Marius were awakened by the scent of burning brush choking the air about them. The mountain was encased in thick black smoke. Marius climbed the short distance to the summit above the cave. His heart froze when he saw the orange glow several miles below him. He climbed back down to where Terra waited. "There's fire moving toward the village!" They quickly prepared to leave to do what they could to help.

Turning back to the cave, they saw the Ancient Mother sitting motionless, her white hair loose and flowing down the back of her shawl. They approached her, and as they reached forward to touch her back, her shawl and hair fell away from their hands and became the shape of alabaster wings, and her face beaked and feathered. She rose up, a magnificent white hawk that circled above them. The hawk called to them, dipping her flashing wings against the dark sky, "Trust yourself. You will know what to do." Terra and Marius followed as she guided them toward the smoldering slope.

Terra and Marius climbed down a narrow trail that led directly through the forest. The path was difficult and slippery, and Terra and Marius leaned many times into the bending willow staff and helped each other across fallen logs and mossy rocks. The smoke often blocked their view, and Terra held her scarf about her mouth and nose to help her breathe. But as they neared the village they could see their path would eventually bring them to the fire.

Finally, just ahead of them stretched the narrow stone bridge to the village. Its planked wooden roadbed was now covered with coals so hot that the heat burned their cheeks and lit the dry brush of the hillside. Behind them the flames leaped across the road and blocked their retreat. Below the river raged. They stopped at the foot of the bridge and, glancing at each other, removed their boots.

Terra stopped and drew inside herself, Marius standing firmly by her side, their hands entwined. Could she cross the fire? She closed her eyes and saw for a moment the swirl of flame in the galaxies and the beauty of that sight, and she heard again the roar of the blaze that brought her to the earth. Her fear vanished in the sure, steady vibration of the crystal deep within.

Terra gazed at Marius. They released hands and bowed to the flames. She was the first to step forward, feeling the crunch of the coals beneath her feet. But there was no heat, only the sensation that her feet were bathed in oil as cool as the waters of the ocean's edge. She moved onward, sparks leaping toward the hem of her dress. Terra kept her eyes on a spot of ground on the other side and walked until she reached it. She thanked the fire for letting her pass and waited for Marius to follow, his gaze never leaving hers as he crossed the coals.

Surrender

The whole village was in the streets carrying food and valuables from their homes. The sudden appearance of Marius and Terra offered a brief moment of hope to the frightened and weary villagers. Marius helped carry the children and elder ones to the harbor. He sang and joked with the little ones who clung to his neck and arms. He placed them gently among the small fleet of boats that had been readied for escape from the fire.

Just ahead of the flames came the forest creatures: deer, rabbits, fox, and owls, darting into the streets of the village, scrambling inside open doorways and startled by the screams of children and frightened horses. Terra calmed the frantic animals with her voice and hands, and led them through the streets to the water's edge. There they huddled in a mass, predator and prey together. Terra smiled to see the loon safely sitting atop a piling on the dock, a bit sooty and disheveled.

The wind brought the scent of burning cedar and ancient oak and hickory. Meanwhile, Marius found his way to where the baker and the other men carried water to soak the roofs of the homes closest to the forest. But it was not long before they knew only rain could save the village.

The baker paused and then, stepping in front of the line of men, faced the oncoming smoke and flames. He began to speak in a clear, strong voice. The others, hearing his words and feeling his calmness, stopped and stood with him.

> *We thank the Great One for our lives.*
> *We thank the Earth for the gifts she gives us.*
> *We thank the Sky for the lightning that sparked these flames*
> *and the rain that will quench it.*
> *We thank the Ocean that will bear us to safety.*
> *And we thank this Fire for what it brings and what it will take away.*
> *We ask for faith in the wisdom of all.*
> *So be it.*

Far above them, slowly circling with her mighty wings spread, the lone white hawk watched, breathing in the waves of fear and smoke as they twisted together in an upward spiral. A single tear escaped from her dark eyes, falling to the ground at the very center of the village. She dipped her wings and disappeared.

The men then turned toward the harbor to launch the loaded boats. As they passed the center of the village they realized the gray air had softened into fog, and a rain was spreading steadily outward. They stopped and stood in wonder as the water streaked their sooty hands and faces. Many of them knelt in gratitude, while others simply wept for joy.

In the hours after the fire Terra and Marius together greeted the villagers, all celebrating their return and good fortune. The baker, seeing the couple together, threw open his doors and passed bread and pies among those gathered.

Families wearily trudged homeward and boats were returned to their moorings. The last of the wild creatures left the harbor, picking their way through smoldering logs and back into the forest and fields. The loon, sitting upon the antlers of a large buck, pointed the deer toward his meadow stream.

Late in the day, Terra found Marius in the back of the bakery, sweeping the floor and straightening the shelves. As she watched, she felt as if she had always been standing there with him while he worked. When he looked up and saw her, he smiled and said, "Are you lost?"

Terra laughed and, reaching for his hand, replied, "Lost? I think not. Come with me."

They walked hand in hand on the familiar path to the cottage, speaking little as they each thought of their new life together. They saw glimpses of what they might teach the other and what they might learn, and how they could give each other courage in the times it was so hard to love and be human. Perhaps she would learn to laugh with the dolphins, and perhaps he would find the healing in his hands, and perhaps they would come to know the full measure of each other's love.

Epilogue

Their silhouettes, seen through the window of the cottage at the place where the meadow meets the sand and the sea, were obscured in the fog. So we may not see their shapes when next they wander the meadow hill. And we may not know their end. But neither can we know the place where the tails of high cirrus clouds grow so wispy they become the darkening blue of the heavens. Neither can we touch the place where the sound of cicadas, stirring the summer air, grows so faint it stops—and the silence of the starry night begins.

Acknowledgments

It takes more than a village to publish a book, especially one that was written over such a long period of time. During this gestation many of you read and commented, loaned me a place to write, referred me to agents and publishers, or just listened and encouraged.

Foremost in my gratitude is my husband, Buck, who has been my constant cheerleader for more than forty years and my mother, Dolores Gurley, who loves everything I write and never misses a spelling error.

Other early readers and supporters included family members Katherine and Max Goldstein, Jon and Joan Gurley, Lily Friedlander, Amy Goldstein, and Sonja Bolle; my Atlanta writing group, Moira Keller, Ginger Birdsey, Betsy Baker, Kelly Richards, and Bev Bradburn-Stern, and in Martha's Vineyard, my dear teacher and inspiration at the Chilmark Writing Workshop, Nancy Aronie, and fellow student Elizabeth Brinckerhoff; and those who added their professional comments to the manuscript over the years: Chuck Perry, Peggy Payne, David Payne, and Jerry Lee Davis. Special shout out to Taylor Brown, who wrote the song "Children of the Stars."

I especially appreciate the comments of my young adult readers, Emma Thorp, Amelia Guttentag, Charlotte Buck, and Daniel Jubelirer, who helped me see this story with new eyes.

Other cheerleaders include Diane Hise, Sharon Benson, Karley Kokinakis, Emily Ellison, Diann Kayah, Kristy Lee, Bonnie Sparling, Martha Caldwell, Terry Vance, Debra Landsberg, Katharine Dahl, Laurel

Goldman, Martha Ciaburri, Gus Kaufman, Aaron Mason, Melinda Lawrence, Mark Smith, Patti Thorp, Aviva Diamond, Lauren Jubelirer, Martha-Elizabeth Ferguson, Beverly Johnston, Bob Forbes, the late Stan Hart, Cliff Graubart, Debbie Jeffress, Megan Wilson, the late Margot Powell, Judith Orloff, Julie Kimball, David Perry, David Kiel, Barbara Croft, Amey Miller, Elaine Kolodkin, Jane Condon, Joan and R. O. Rushton, Nathalie Dupree, Judy Tabb, Rhalee Hughes, Elaine Silverstein, John Haber, Susan Taylor and Nick Taylor, whose wise advice about the publishing world has been a huge help.

I am grateful for the encouragement and skills of editor Jan Pogue (and her team, including book designer Jill Dible) at Vineyard Stories, for making a home for *Star Child* and midwiving the story into print.

Special appreciation to my meditation students, especially the Wednesday morning group whose journeys have taught me so much: Chuck, Amy, Kathy, Ann, Suzanne, Lucia, Magda, Jeff, Matt, Kurt, Mary and colleague, Mary Love May.

My gratitude to all of my teachers, seen and unseen, and especially those whose earthly lessons have brought me closer to spirit: Leong Tan, Meg McLaughlin, Mike Flowers, Neala Peake, Danielle Gibbons, Forrest Green.

K Goldstein

About the Author

Kay Goldstein is a cook, writer and teacher of meditation who was delighted to find herself writing a story about star children. She is the co-author of *A Book of Feasts, Stories and Recipes from American Celebrations* and has been a regular contributor to the Huffington Post and her own blog at www.lessonsforthecook.com. Kay is married to Buck Goldstein, and they have two children, Katherine and Max. She divides her time between Chapel Hill, North Carolina, and Martha's Vineyard, Massachusetts.

www.thestarchildbook.com
www.lessonsforthecook.com
Follow Kay on twitter@chefshaman
Look for Star Child on Facebook

A portion of all proceeds from the sale of this book will support preservation of natural habitats in Martha's Vineyard and elsewhere.